D0704352

ANCIENT EGYPT
◁ MYTHS AND LEGENDS ▷

Translated by Abigail Frost

Illustrated by Jean-Marie Ruffieux, Jean-Jacques and Yves Chagnaud

Original version by Alain Quesnel

Edited by Gilles Ragache

CHERRYTREE BOOKS

A Cherrytree Book

Adapted by A S Publishing
from *L'Egypte*
published by Hachette

First published 1989
by Cherrytree Press Ltd
a subsidiary of
The Chivers Company Ltd
Windsor Bridge Road
Bath, Avon BA2 3AX

Reprinted 1991, 1992 (twice), 1993

First softcover edition 1994

Reprinted 1995

British Library Cataloguing in Publication Data
Quesnel, Alain
    Ancient Egypt. (Myths and legends (Cherrytree
    Books)).
    1. Myths. Legends. Egyptian myths. Egyptian legends.
    Egyptian myths and legends, ancient period
    I. Title   II. Frost, Abigail   III. Ruffieux, Jean-
    Marie   IV. Chagnaud, Jean-Jacques   V. Chagnaud, Yves
    VI. L'Egypte. *English*
    398.2'0932

    ISBN 0-7451-5058-6 (Hardcover)
    ISBN 0-7451-5241-4 (Softcover)

Printed in Hong Kong by Colorcraft Ltd

▷ CONTENTS ◁

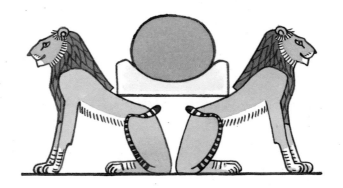

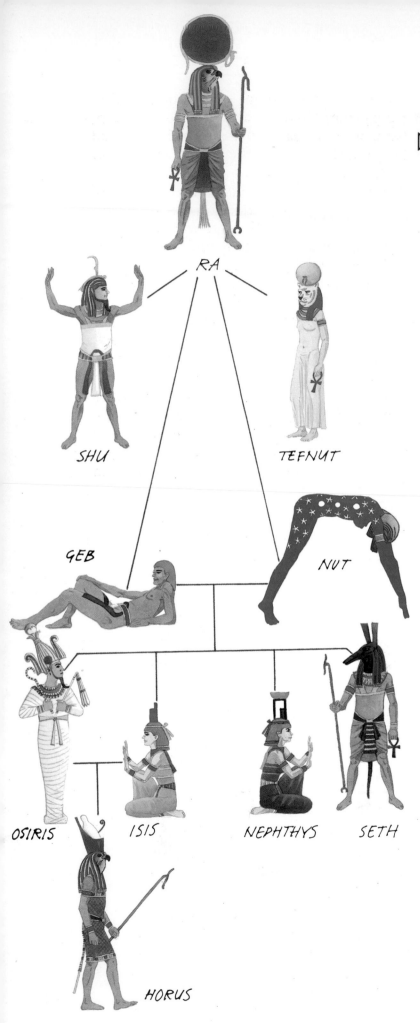

RA

SHU

TEFNUT

GEB

NUT

OSIRIS

ISIS

NEPHTHYS

SETH

HORUS

This book is about the stories of the people and gods of Ancient Egypt: a land where you could stand with one foot in a green field and the other in desert sand. The River Nile, which runs the length of Egypt, flooded once a year and covered its banks with rich, fertile mud where crops could grow. Without the floods there would have been no people, and no stories, because there would have been no food. The Egyptians, thousands of years ago, realised this, and were grateful to the Nile. They hailed its god, Hapi, as 'Bringer of food, rich in provisions, creator of all good, lord of majesty'.

Egypt was two united countries: Lower Egypt, or the Delta, where the Nile split into many little streams on its way to the Mediterra-

THOTH   ANUBIS

nean Sea, and Upper Egypt, along the length of the main river. Upper Egypt had a vulture-goddess called Nekhbet, and Lower Egypt a cobra-goddess, Ouadjyt. The whole country was ruled by kings called pharaohs, who were themselves believed to be gods.

The Egyptians worshipped many strange gods, and it is sometimes difficult to work out which is which. The most obviously strange thing about them is that nearly all were shown in pictures and statues with the heads of animals; sometimes in the legends they switch between human and animal heads, or change themselves completely into animals. The goddess Hathor, for instance, could be a beautiful woman, a woman with a cow's head, or a cow who fed baby gods with her milk.

The greatest of the Egyptian gods was Ra, god of the sun, and father of all the other gods. He went by many names, which differed according to the places where he was worshipped and different aspects of the sun. Amon-Ra is a name for him as the great national god of Egypt. Ra's children, according to the Egyptians, were the earth, the air and the sky, and his grandchildren were the chief gods of Egypt.

Other gods represented things the Egyptians thought important. Thoth was the god of wisdom and the inventor of the Egyptians' picture-writing. Anubis, a god with the head of a jackal, was a god of death and funerals. The Egyptians believed in another world where people went after death, and took great care to prepare for it. They preserved dead bodies as mummies, built magnificent tombs, and filled them with the dead person's possessions and models of the things he or she would need in the next world.

There were many lesser gods who looked after particular places, and friendly gods who were worshipped at home by ordinary people rather than in great temples full of learned priests. We shall meet some of them at the end of the book.

NEKHBET   OUADJYT

HATHOR

5

▷ THE BIRTH OF THE WORLD ◁

Nobody knows how our world was born. In Egypt people said that at the very beginning there was nothing but an ocean without shores, whose waves rolled and broke in the shadows. Then, little by little, at the bottom of the waters there rose a mass of sand and mud. An island emerged from the sea.

On this tiny island appeared a smooth and perfect egg. And when it hatched, there was the sun god Ra, who filled the universe with his dazzling light. Ra soon began to create and organize the world, with his own children. His daughter Nut was goddess of the sky. She bent her vast and star-studded body above the earth.

In the middle Ra's son Shu, the air, held up Nut's stomach to make the arch of the sky and separate her from the earth. Finally, Khonsou, god of the moon, ruled the night skies, when Ra went to the underworld.

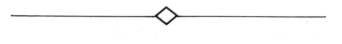

SEKHMET'S HUNT

Those miserable creatures, men, were upsetting Ra, with complaints and cries of rebellion. The army of rebels grew bigger each day. Fools! How could the father of the gods fear them?

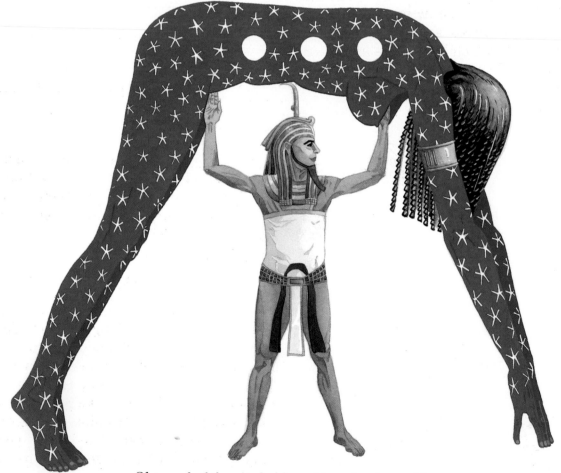

Shu, god of the air, holds up Nut, the sky-goddess.

'Ra, worried by their ingratitude, called the other gods and asked for their advice. They said he should show the rebels the terrible wrath of his eye.

Ra's eye could leave his body and move about as a powerful god in its own right. It usually went into the world in the form of the peaceful cow-goddess called Hathor, but when angry it became the terrifying Sekhmet, a goddess with a woman's body and the head of a lioness.

This bloodthirsty goddess threw herself on the rebellious men and sowed terror in their ranks. She slew them in great numbers, the innocent with the guilty.

This massacre enraged Ra: he had wanted to quell the revolt, but not to wipe out human life. He ordered Sekhmet to stop at once, but she refused and continued the hunt.

The wise Ra waited for the night and the moment when Sekhmet, exhausted by her ravages, fell asleep. Then he made a drink for her, from magic herbs and the red juice of pomegranates, to which he added a little of her victims' blood. This he mixed with a lot of beer – enough to fill 700 pitchers. Then silently his servants took this drink to the sleeping hun-

Ra, the sun-god, sometimes shown with a hawk's head.

Hathor, the cow-goddess, one form of the eye of Ra.

tress. Sekhmet awoke thirsty, and drank Ra's potion greedily. She staggered away drunkenly, and forgot all about her hunt. To make sure she never killed again, Ra commanded people to make regular peace-offerings of beer to Sekhmet.

◇

NO MORE HUMAN SACRIFICE

Then there was more killing in Egypt. The men who had been loyal to Ra, hoping to please him, executed those rebels Sekhmet had not killed. This was a just punishment, according to the ways of the time, but Ra was a peaceful god and human sacrifice disgusted him. He ordered that in future, when a man offended the gods, an animal, such as a bull, gazelle or bird, should be sacrificed in his place.

▷ THE BARGE OF THE SUN ◁

The Egyptians believed that dawn broke when Ra opened his eyelids. Night fell when he shut them. He woke in the east, where two gods dressed him and led him to his golden barge. The vessel set forth silently over the celestial ocean. All day it crossed the sky, giving the world light and warmth.

WORLDS UNDERGROUND

As the skies darkened, Ra's barge sailed out of the world we can see. The god exchanged his human daytime face for the horned head of a ram, while his barge crossed the savage and lonely region which separated the kingdoms of the living and the dead. He passed through the twelve gates of night, each representing an hour.

At last Ra landed in the underworld. He went to greet Osiris, who reigned over the dead. The dead waited on the bank to cheer the god and tow his boat. Then the sun god went down to the caverns of the west, which were totally dark; even Ra, with his magic eye, could see nothing there. The river was infested with snakes, and Ra had to use magic to pass. Some Egyptians said that he changed his barge into a

Ra's battle with the dreadful serpent Apopis was the climax of his nightly journey.

Ra's barge as shown in a tomb painting.

huge serpent which easily passed through the swarming reptiles. Others thought he placed himself under the protection of a sacred serpent.

Once these dangers were passed, the barge would move on with stately ease. Two fish, one pink and one blue, swam ahead. Suddenly they would give the alarm: Ra's greatest enemy was near.

Ahead loomed the huge, threatening silhouette of the serpent Apopis. Every morning and evening this gigantic monster attacked Ra. If Apopis ever won, the sun would disappear and the universe would be plunged into chaos. It would mean the end of the world, the death of the earth, the stars and the planets.

Ra used all his magic powers in the battle. Sometimes as they fought Apopis's colossal body would hide Ra from sight, causing an eclipse of the sun. Ra always triumphed, but the monster, never discouraged by defeat, returned to fight every day. Ra's victory was the climax of his nightly journey. The sun passed through a monumental gate back into the world of the living. And dawn broke once more, bringing joy to everyone.

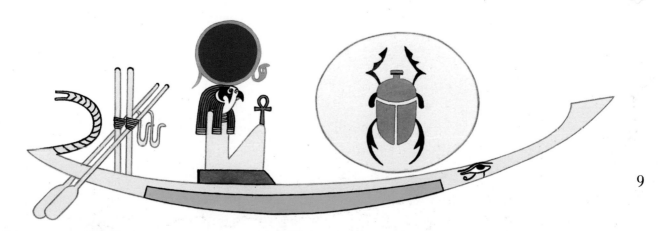

▷ THE WORDS OF THE GODS ◁

The wise god was sometimes represented as an ibis . . . sometimes as a baboon.

Thoth was always dreaming up new inventions.

The god Thoth was called 'Lord of the voice' and 'master of words'. This wise god was master of all knowledge, even the most mysterious. Even Ra, when he was feeling old, tired and ill, called on the god to make him better.

This wise and healing god was worshipped at many temples, particularly at Hermopolis. Sometimes he was represented in pictures and statues as an ibis, sometimes as a big white baboon. He was always dreaming up new inventions. After creating all the languages of the earth, he was said to have invented numbers, arithmetic, geometry and astronomy. He found ways to measure time, and invented the first calendar. His fertile mind thought up the games of chess and dice. But one particular idea obsessed him. Life would be so much easier if there were a way to put down our thoughts so that everyone could share and understand them. Thoth mulled the problem over and at last he solved it. The ibis god invented writing. Of course, his inventions would be no use if he kept them to himself. Thoth wanted them to help all the people.

He went down to the royal city of Thebes to see Amon-Ra. He told the king of the gods all about his discoveries, and how they would help his people. Amon listened carefully, and asked for many explanations. This invention sounded useful to him, that one was unnecessary . . . At last the conversation came round to writing.

'It's the best of all my ideas,' said Thoth. 'The Egyptians will be able to learn so much, and keep all their knowledge for ever! Writing will kill ignorance and cure bad memories.'

But Amon disagreed. 'I think you're wrong. Your great invention will be a bad thing. If people don't use their memories, they will

forget everything. If they can write, they will not bother to remember things, because it will be so much easier to use written words. And again, they will think themselves fit to do all sorts of things that, without writing, they could not possibly do. You will give them only false, superficial knowledge.' But in spite of Amon's doubts, in the end all Thoth's inventions were given to the people of Egypt.

THOTH'S DISCIPLES

An old tree cast a huge shadow over the courtyard at Amon-Ra's temple. In this sacred place, Thoth and the goddess Seschat, 'mistress of writing and queen of the house of books', worked at a strange task: writing on the tree's leaves the names of all the kings of Egypt. The Egyptians followed their gods' example and wrote down all the important events of history, and the small events of everyday life. Those who knew writing – the words of the god – were well respected and powerful. Scribes, the people who wrote things down, were Thoth's earthly fellows.

Every father dreamed of his son growing up to be a scribe. An old scholar took his son to school to begin the long, hard years of study which would enable him to become a scribe in the pharaoh's palace. Before they parted, the old man gave the boy this advice:

'My son, put all your heart into your books. Love them like your mother, for there is nothing more important. Every career has its troubles and miseries. Only the learned man who follows Thoth in the noble career of letters will know deep and lasting happiness.'

Pepi, the son, never forgot his father's advice, which the teachers at school repeated too. He would rather become a scribe than take up the dangerous life of a soldier or the hard life of a farmer. At the end of his education, Pepi went to work in the royal civil service. There, under a statue of a white baboon, he worked hard and never forgot to honour Thoth, the scribe of the gods. People treated Pepi as an important man, keeper of secret wisdom.

HIEROGLYPHS

We use an alphabet in which letters stand for the sounds that make up words. The Egyptians used hieroglyphs, a sort of writing made up of pictures, for their sacred texts. This did not mean that a picture of an animal, say, always stood for the name of the animal; it might represent an idea associated with it, such as courage, or the sound of a word or part of a word. Not everything you might wish to write down can be shown in a picture. Hieroglyphs were carved in stone, painted on walls or engraved on jewels; they appeared anywhere an inscription was wanted. But most everyday documents were written on papyrus, a material made from reeds. The word gives us our word, paper.

▷ ISIS AND OSIRIS ◁

The universe trembled with Ra's anger. The crippled old god shook with indignation at the news. His daughter Nut, the sky, and Geb, the earth, had defied his orders by getting married. The furious father of the gods cursed the couple. His curse was that they could not have children on any day of the year. Nut, who longed for children, was miserable.

Then she had an idea. She challenged Thoth, who measured the hours, to a game of dice. By clever tricks, Nut beat the ibis-god, and could choose her prize. She asked Thoth to add five days to the Egyptian year, which, until then, had had only 360 days. Ra had no control over the new days, because they were not on the calendar. During these secret days, without her father's knowledge, Nut could have babies.

A KING IS BORN

Months passed by. Then one day in Thebes, a brave man entered the temple in search of water. All alone in the huge building he heard a deep and powerful voice from the shadows announce that Nut's son, Osiris, greatest of kings, had come into the world to bring it great gifts. The first of Thoth's five secret days had come to pass. The voice predicted a great destiny for Osiris, but great sorrows, too.

In the days that followed Nut had three more children: Seth, the red-headed god, and two daughters, Isis and Nephthys. Ra's curse had failed. The sun god resigned himself to it and, tired of earthly matters, he retired to the sky. He left the throne of Egypt to Osiris, who married his sister Isis. Seth married Nephthys, and reigned over the great desert and its scattered oases. From the start, the brothers Seth and Osiris were rivals.

THE GIFTS OF THE GOD

Isis and Osiris governed Egypt from their palace at Thebes. Until they came the people had been poor and uncivilized; some say that, because they could not defend or feed themselves properly, they were cannibals. Isis at once forbade this dreadful practice. She taught the people how to live peacefully in families,

Osiris sets out to conquer the world, with Thoth and Anubis at his side.

and all about the art of medicine. With Nephthys's help, she taught them other useful arts: how to weave cloth and how to make bread with one of Osiris's gifts: corn.

As god of the plant world, Osiris showed his people the plants which would feed them: corn, grapes and barley. He forged the first hoe and built the first plough with his own hands, and taught the Egyptians how to use them. They learned how to sow, reap and grind the grain; how to press grapes to make wine; and how to make beer from barley. Osiris showed his subjects how to extract gold, copper and iron from the earth. With these metals the Egyptians could make arms to defend themselves and tools for their work.

Finally, Osiris organized their religion; he taught them the correct way to worship the gods and built many temples in great cities. Not content with civilizing the Egyptians, Osiris rode all over the great world accompanied by Thoth and Anubis, the jackal-headed god. He conquered other lands peacefully and shared his gifts with their people.

Under the firm and kindly rule of Isis and Osiris, life was sweet for the Egyptians. They gave thanks to their rulers, particularly Osiris, whom they called the Good One.

▷ SETH'S TREACHERY ◁

Gathered around the red-headed god Seth was a rabble of conspirators, preparing to commit a terrible crime. Their words were full of bitterness; they could not bear the happiness of Egypt. They hated Osiris for bringing order and justice to the land, and were jealous of his subjects' faithful love. For many years, in the shadow of his elder brother, Seth had raged inside. The desert had been his share of the world, while fertile Egypt went to Osiris. And his jealousy had grown with time. Seth had one ambition: to usurp his brother's throne. He spied on the least things Osiris did, waiting for the right moment to carry out his wicked plan. To help him, he had sworn in 72 conspirators, all mortal enemies of Osiris.

Now, Osiris had returned to his kingdom after a long journey. Happy to see his lands again, the kindly god had made a stop at the town of Memphis. Seth ran to meet him with honeyed words of welcome, and an invitation to a great feast in his honour. As he talked and embraced his brother, Seth secretly took Osiris's measurements. Later he took them to a carpenter and ordered him to make a wooden chest, richly decorated and beautifully worked.

At the hour of the banquet, Osiris entered a vast room where Seth and his accomplices greeted him. When the festivities were well under way the precious chest was brought in. Seth announced a competition: whoever fitted perfectly inside it would win the beautiful chest. The plotters pretended to take part. Each in turn stretched out in the chest but it was always too large.

Now it was the tall Osiris's turn to play the game. He lay down in the box with good humour. With wild cries of delight, his enemies threw themselves on the chest and closed the heavy lid. Then they sealed it up with molten lead. Seth gave the word and the chest – now a coffin – was thrown into the waters of the Nile. Slowly the body of the good and just god floated to faraway shores.

Seth took his throne and cruelly persecuted the dead king's friends. Thoth, Anubis, and other gods changed themselves into the shapes of animals to hide from his cruelty. Isis shed bitter tears over her husband's unhappy fate. But she had to think of her own safety, because she was expecting the heir to the kingdom, Osiris's child. Thoth advised her to hide herself in the Nile Delta. And so the goddess fled with seven scorpions as her only companions.

A GODDESS'S KINDNESS

One day, tired after a long walk under blistering sun, Isis approached a house and asked for hospitality. But the woman who lived there was frightened by the scorpions and fiercely chased her away. As Isis left, the scorpion Tefen slid under the door and bit the hard-hearted woman's little son. Its bite was fatal. The woman cried piteously at her terrible loss. Isis, far away, heard her crying, and could not ignore the distress of a fellow mother. She returned and asked the grieving woman to let her see the dead child. In the house, she placed her hands on the little body, and by her charms drew out Tefen's poison. The child came back to life.

The goddess continued her journey to escape Seth. After many long days on the march, at last she reached the marshes of the Delta, and came to a place called Chemnis, near the town of Buto. There she gave birth to her son Horus, who had the head of a falcon. She gave him to the cobra-goddess, Ouadjyt, who ruled the Delta, to bring up in safety.

With wild cries of delight, Osiris's enemies closed the heavy lid.

14

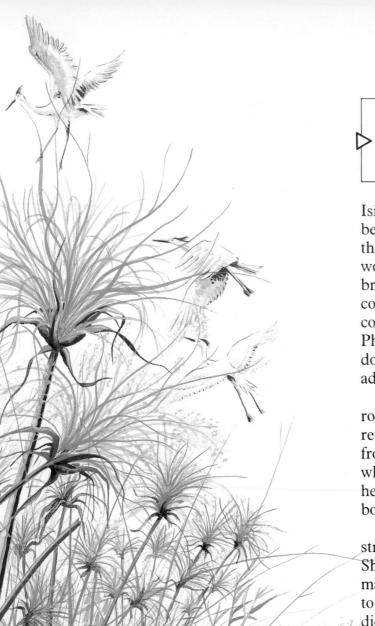

IN SEARCH OF OSIRIS

Isis set out to find Osiris's body. His coffin had been washed up on the Phoenician coast, and the god's dead body had worked a miracle. The wood of the coffin had come to life, growing branches with dizzying speed. Soon all that could be seen was a leafy acacia tree, which completely hid the coffin from sight. When the Phoenician king saw this fine tree, he had it cut down and made into a beautiful column to adorn his palace.

A lonely swallow came to the palace. It flew round and round the column, with heart-rending little cries. It was Isis, who had flown from Egypt in the guise of a bird and found out where Osiris lay. There was only one thing on her mind: how could she get her husband's body back?

People in the town soon noticed a mysterious stranger; it was Isis, now back in human form. She soon met the queen's maids, gossiped and made friends with them, and taught them how to paint their eyes and braid their hair as she did. Soon the beautiful foreigner was the talk of

Isis sailed around the branching Delta streams. . .

the palace; the maids spoke of nothing else. The queen, curious, made them bring Isis to her. She was charmed by the goddess, and made her nurse to her baby son.

Isis lived for many months at the palace, making her plans in secret. One night the queen went to her son's room to look at him as he slept. O horror! The sleeping child was bathed in flames, and seven huge scorpions watched. The queen's screams woke the entire household.

Isis slipped in with the terrified crowd. Raising her hand to break her spell, she said sadly: 'Why didn't you trust me, O Queen? Now your son will not be immortal! The flames were magic, to make him live for ever, but you have spoilt the charm!'

Imagine the king and queen's sorrow! The stranger they had taken into their home was a powerful goddess. So, hoping to regain her favour, the king offered Isis anything she desired. Isis asked for the pillar of acacia wood. She had hardly stopped speaking when it was cut down by the king's command. The goddess tore open the great trunk to find Osiris's coffin inside. Then she put the body in a boat, and sailed for Egypt. She hid the body in the reeds of the Delta, and returned for a while to Buto to see her son Horus.

THE RESURRECTION OF OSIRIS

Isis had a dreadful shock when she came back from Buto. An evil pig had found Osiris's body and shown Seth its hiding-place. The traitor tore the corpse into fourteen pieces and scattered them over the Delta.

Isis almost despaired. But the brave goddess's love was so strong that nothing could stop her. She built a frail reed canoe and sailed around the branching Delta streams, gathering the parts of Osiris's body as she found them. But, sadly, the fourteenth part had been eaten by a fish called an oxyrhynchus. The Egyptians thought the fish unclean for ever after, and would never eat it.

Isis and Nephthys began to put the body back together. Then they prayed to Ra, who sent Thoth and Anubis to help. Anubis, whose secret arts could stop dead bodies decaying, embalmed Osiris with magic potions and wrapped him in bandages. Isis wrote magic spells on them. Then she and Nephthys, transformed into birds, flew up and fanned the corpse with their wings. After a while Osiris opened his eyes.

The murdered god had woken to a new life. He could not return to life on earth. But Ra gave him a new kingdom, the land of the dead. He ruled the dead as wisely as he had the living.

▷ THE VENGEANCE OF HORUS ◁

The child fell down with a howl of pain, breaking the reeds in his fall. The scorpion which had bitten him fled. When his mother returned from the town and found his lifeless body she cried out in horror . . . A cruel new misfortune had hit Isis: Horus was dead! The goddess and her sister prayed to Ra for help. In the shining sky, the sun god stopped his boat's course. Ra sent Thoth to the earth. The ibis-headed god succeeded in reviving Horus, using all his secret knowledge.

At Chemnis, where he was hidden from Seth, life was hard for Horus. He was fed with milk from the cow Hathor, and protected by the cobra Ouadjyt, but the young falcon-god had to face a multitude of difficulties and dangers. First fever devoured him, then his eyes gave him pain. Reptiles and scorpions attacked him and brush fires endangered his life. But despite all these troubles, he grew up and was educated.

THE BATTLE OF THE GODS

When Horus was old enough, Osiris returned briefly to earth. He gave his son weapons and taught him how to fight. Horus, who burned with desire to avenge his father and drive out the usurper Seth, learnt these lessons in war quickly. As soon as he felt ready, he called together the Egyptians who were loyal to Osiris and, encouraged by Isis, declared war on the dreadful tyrant Seth. Seth rallied his troops, and they all changed into a variety of animals: crocodiles, serpents, hippopotamuses and gazelles. Many times the two sides clashed in violent battles but neither side was ever outright winner.

Then came the final confrontation. The two armies met near Edfu in a bloody battle. The clash of arms and deafening war-cries filled the air. Horus took the shape of a falcon and flew up into the heavens. With his piercing eye he searched the confusion of battle. Suddenly he saw Seth, in the shape of a hippopotamus. From high in the sky, Horus fell upon Seth and plunged his hard, sharp claws into his enemy's armoured hide. Taken by surprise, Seth reacted fast, changing into a gazelle and running away. Horus pursued him and they fought one-to-one – a ferocious, merciless battle which was often interrupted but always began again. The two gods attacked each other with cruel and merciless blows. Gravely wounded by Horus, Seth managed to rip out his enemy's eye. But neither

could gain the advantage; the battle seemed likely to go on for ever.

All the gods who were present agreed that it was time to end the battle. They called the two sides together and proposed that Thoth should judge the case. The ibis god told the enemies to dress their wounds and then present their own cases, one after the other. Seth spoke first, saying that Horus was not the true heir of Osiris, because he was born after his father's death. Then Horus made an eloquent speech, showing that Seth was wrong; he was the true son of Isis and Osiris and had the right to the throne. Then he reminded the court of his uncle's crimes. The gods withdrew to decide. Thoth wanted to give Horus his father's king-dom; Geb suggested dividing the land, so that Horus would rule the Delta and Seth the Nile Valley. No one knows exactly how the gods decided, but in the end Egypt was reunited under Horus's rule.

Horus ruled wisely, just like his father. After him, his descendants reigned. The first was Menes, the first pharaoh of Egypt. For more than 3000 years, the rulers of the 27 dynasties of Egypt were believed to be the heirs of Horus.

Seth lived on, brooding about his defeat. He kept repeating in his mind his battle against Horus – the war of the forces of darkness against those of the light. The deep respect the Egyptians held for Horus was matched only by their fear of Seth.

The battle of the gods: Horus the falcon against Seth the hippopotamus.

19

▷ ISIS PLAYS A TRICK ◁

A wretched old man hobbled about the heavens, almost crippled. It was the god Ra, powerful lord of the skies and master of the universe. Time had mastered him, as it does us all. Not even great Ra could escape old age. Gods and humans worried as he grew feebler each day and the sun's light faded. Ra's limbs became stiff, his bones were changing to silver. Gradually his body was turning to gold and his hair to lapis lazuli, a bright blue gemstone. Soon the sun would be a cold mass of metal and stone.

Among Ra's many children and grandchildren was Isis, who had become a great sorceress. She knew all there was to know about the sky, the earth and the underworld. But there was one thing she did not know – something which would give her immense power: the true name of Ra.

Isis brought the little snake to life . . .

The sun god was known by many names: Ptah, Amon, Atum . . . men and gods knew him by these names and more. But Ra jealously hid his true name – the name which he alone had heard. This name had great magical powers, which Isis coveted. Seeing Ra, grey and bent over his stick, the wise and cunning goddess made a plan.

THE MAGIC SERPENT

Every day Ra took a walk, hobbling along the same path. Isis spied on him from behind thick bushes. One day the old god cleared his throat and spat as he passed. When he had moved away, the sorceress went to where his spittle had fallen, and mixed it with soil. With this mud she modelled a snake, and hid it on Ra's usual path. Then, with magic words, she brought the clay snake to life.

Ra went out as usual on his walk. Suddenly he felt a sharp pain in his foot, which soon spread through his body. He did not see the little snake dart away. One minute he felt burning hot, the next icy cold. He shivered and cried out in pain.

All the gods came running at his cry, and listened as he said he was suffering from an unknown illness. The great sun god was powerless in the face of pain.

Then Isis came forward from the crowd of gods. 'Divine Father,' she said. 'You have been

All the gods came running at Ra's cry . . .

bitten by a snake. Its burning poison is causing your agony.' She waited a little, then added: 'Reveal your real name to me, and I will make a spell to take the pain away.' Faint with pain, the old god writhed on the ground. But still he hesitated, not wanting to give anything away. He began to list all his earthly names:

'In the morning I am Khephri, Ra at noon, and Atum in the evening . . .' But Isis was not fooled, and retorted:

'None of these names is your true name. Tell me that and my magic will cure you!'

Ra's suffering was unbearable, and at last he gave in, calling Isis to his side:

'Here! I will pour into your heart the power that is in mine!' The goddess and the sick god moved away, where others could not hear. Reluctantly, he whispered in her ear his mysterious true name. Isis spoke magic words to break her own spell. Ra immediately felt well again, but soon felt angry with himself for giving away the secret of his power. But Isis was happy; now she was one of the greatest of the gods.

▷ THE TEMPLE OF EDFU ◁

Horus, the great sky-god with the head of a falcon, had a magnificent temple in his honour in the south of Upper Egypt, about 100 kilometres from Luxor. The temple, which was built between about 237 and 57 BC, was a replacement for a much older one. It is one of the best-preserved monuments of Ancient Egypt. The temple is part of a huge complex of buildings, most of which have not yet been excavated.

This temple is not even the biggest of Egyptian religious buildings. There are much larger ones at Karnak and Luxor. But it has some unusual features. It is the only temple built facing south, for example.

Inside the temple the architects have created subtle effects of light and shade. Worshippers went from a sunny courtyard into dark mysterious halls. The building grew darker as they approached the holy of holies, Horus's sanctuary.

5 *Chapel of the bull-god Min.*

6 *The great sanctuary, where the god's statue was kept. Only a few priests were allowed to enter.*

7 *Around the temple was a great corridor. On its high outside walls were reliefs showing Horus's battle with Seth.*

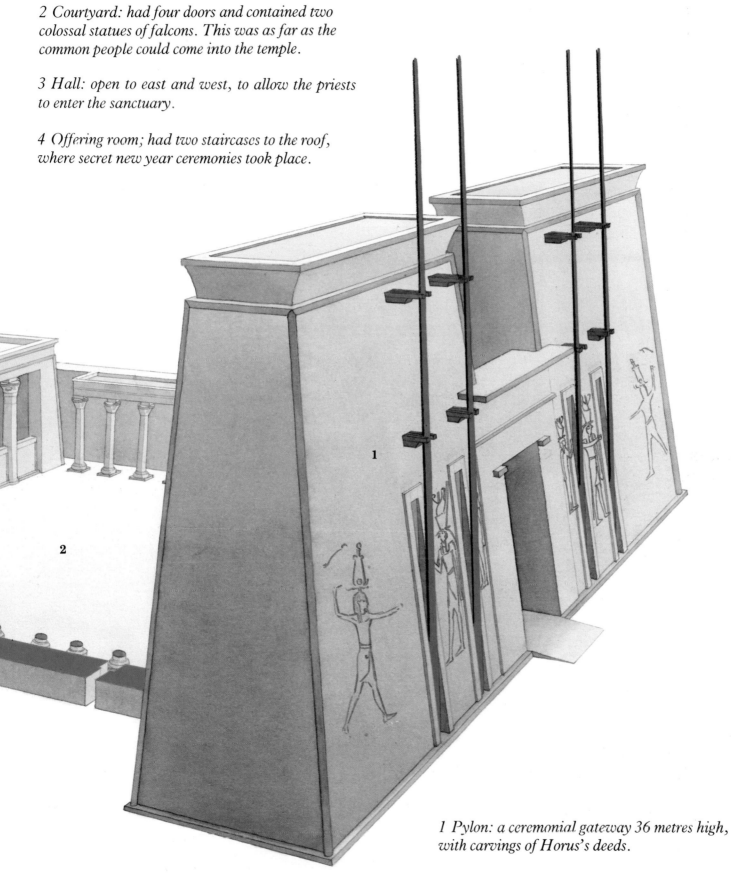

2 Courtyard: had four doors and contained two colossal statues of falcons. This was as far as the common people could come into the temple.

3 Hall: open to east and west, to allow the priests to enter the sanctuary.

4 Offering room; had two staircases to the roof, where secret new year ceremonies took place.

1 Pylon: a ceremonial gateway 36 metres high, with carvings of Horus's deeds.

▷ EGYPTIAN RELIGION ◁

As dawn broke over Thebes the temple of Amon-Ra was bustling. All the priests hurried to open the sanctuary, the most secret of their holy places, which was forbidden to the public. It held the god's image, a tiny statue in a model barge. The statue stood in a cabin shaped like a temple, draped with curtains. The barge was decorated with the heads of rams, which were sacred to the sun-god.

The priests sang a morning hymn as the god woke up. They placed food offerings before the statue, and left Amon-Ra to enjoy his breakfast. They came back to wash the god, paint him with fresh make-up and change his clothes. Then they adorned and perfumed him. Once Amon-Ra had everything he needed, they made more offerings to lesser gods. Then they shared the food the gods had left among themselves and the temple staff. At the noon service, they

sprinkled the sanctuary with holy water and burnt incense. The evening service was like the morning one, getting the god ready for bed. When he went to sleep, the priests purified the temple, closed it up and went to bed.

All the ceremonies were secret: ordinary people could not look at the image of the god. But there were many festivals which they could join in, to celebrate the beginning of a new year or season, the sowing and harvest of crops, the Nile floods, or royal occasions such as a coronation. Some festivals lasted as long as a month.

In the fourth month of the Egyptian year came a ceremony which was celebrated all over Egypt: the one which marked the rebirth of Osiris. The god's barge was carried in a great procession from the temple into the town. The people could come near the god, but not see

him, because he was hidden behind veils.

TELLING FORTUNES

When the god left his temple to move among the crowd, the people had an opportunity to obtain his advice about the future. All you had to do was stand near the passing barge and watch it. If the barge-carriers went forward, the god approved of what you wanted to do; if they went back, he did not. Oracles were another way to get a god's opinion. If you had a problem, you could ask him what to do and draw from a container one of many answers written on a clay tablet or a piece of reed. Amon-Ra's temple at Thebes, Isis's at Coptos and Bes's at Abydos all had famous oracles. You could also get the god's advice by spending the night in a temple. Your problems were solved in your dreams.

Dreams were also a way to find out the future. Scribes interpreted them according to a long list of meanings. A man who dreamed he saw himself at the bottom of a pit would be imprisoned; one who met a dwarf in his dream would die young. If you dreamed of looking out of a window, it meant the god would hear your call and answer it.

The Egyptian people believed strongly in magic. They kept amulets (good-luck charms) to ward off evil. Evil spirits were often pictured stabbed with knives to stop them doing harm. Magic calmed people's fears.

There were religious ceremonies connected with farming. The Nile was life itself for the Egyptians, who honoured its god Hapi. When the annual floods rose and watered the land, people met at the 'house of Hapi' and threw cakes, fruit and amulets into the river to feed the kindly god. Another ceremony helped plants grow. People made a rough statue of Osiris from clay mixed with grains. In a few days the grains sprouted, and Osiris would make the crops grow.

Just like the state religion, these ceremonies and superstitions show us something about the Egyptians' joys and sorrows, hopes and fears.

Every year a fleet of decorated boats took Amon-Ra's statue from his temple at Karnak to another at Luxor.

▷ PHARAOH, SON OF RA ◁

It was rare for an ordinary Egyptian to be allowed into the presence of the pharaoh – a god. Anyone so privileged had first to pay homage at the foot of the throne by 'smelling the earth', as the Egyptians called it. The king was always richly dressed, the image of beauty and perfection. He wore an animal's tail for a belt, a false beard, and carried a sceptre. These were symbols to show that the pharaoh was not a man, but a true living god. His crown – called the pschent – itself was worshipped fervently. It was red and white, the colours of the two lands which made up Egypt. Royal crowns had supernatural powers, and could only be touched by specially initiated people. They were not just hats, but signs of the gods' power. So they were treated with respect; people even sang hymns to them. On the pharaoh's forehead was a jewel shaped like a cobra, its 'hood' raised

in anger. This was the serpent Uraeus, the goddess of flames, who represented the powerful eye of Ra.

The pharaoh, according to the Egyptians, was not born in the same way as ordinary men. Ra knew who he would be long before his birth. When the time came, Ra took the form of the reigning pharaoh and made love to his queen, so that he was the real father of the future ruler. Khnoum, the ram-headed god, made a pottery model of the child to be and of his invisible double, his Ka. Heket, a goddess with a frog's face, blew life into these little clay people with her magic breath. Heket and Khnoum helped at the birth. All the gods cried out with joy when the baby was born. Like Horus, he was fed with the cow-goddess Hathor's milk.

The baby grew into a boy, then a man. At last the day came when his earthly father, the

pharaoh, died. Then his heavenly father, Ra, introduced him to the other gods at his coronation. The coronation was a grand ceremony, which took place under the eye of the gods – represented on earth by their statues. Seth and Horus gave him the crowns of Upper and Lower Egypt, to make him lord over the whole country, like all the pharaohs before him.

As he performed his royal duties, the pharaoh never forgot his ancestors, that long line of gods who had reigned in past times and now lay in their pyramids. He had his own pyramid built, ready for the day when he too would return to live among the gods beside Ra. In life, he arranged for companions in death – he let his favourite courtiers build their own tombs at the foot of his pyramid, so they would be nearby. He granted his friends immortality like his own, in the kingdom of Osiris. The death of a pharaoh was no ordinary event; to the Egyptians, it was like an eclipse of the sun, darkening the world until the sun returned in the form of the new pharaoh.

Horus, in falcon form, hovers over the pharaoh to protect him in war.

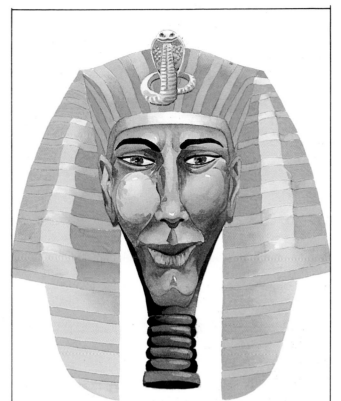

AKHENATEN, THE REBEL KING

One pharaoh was different from all the others. Amenophis IV (1364-1347 BC) had angry disputes with the priests of Amon-Ra, who had great power. He decided to abolish their religion and worship instead a single god: Aten, the disc of the sun. Aten was pictured as a disc with rays coming from it; the rays ended in hands, which gave gifts to the king and his wife. The king also changed his name, from Amenophis ('Amon is pleased') to Akhenaten ('He who pleases Aten'), and moved his capital to a new town, Akhetaton. He had all the images and even the name of Amon-Ra destroyed. But his new religion, imposed by force, did not last long after his death. Under the next king, Tutankhamun, all the images of Aten were destroyed, and Amon-Ra returned to his temple. Akhenaten's mummy, and his wife's, were hidden away in a secret tomb, so that the angry priests could not harm them.

27

At dead of night Sinhue left his native land.

SINHUE'S ADVENTURE

The man's heart was beating fit to burst as he hid in the bushes. The slightest movement might give him away. It was dark night, but he still feared being seen by the sentry.

Suddenly he stood up and ran as fast as he could, vanishing into the darkness before the soldiers saw him. Sinhue had crossed the Eastern frontier. He had left Egypt, his homeland, where he faced certain death. Ahead lay unknown lands. Who could tell what dangers might await him there?

Sinhue had no choice. He had been on the pharaoh's staff, and fought beside Prince Sesostris, the pharaoh's son and heir, in his wars. But the pharaoh had died, and his other sons kept his death a secret, while they tried to get the throne for themselves. Sinhue was one of the few to know the truth. He feared for his life – there would surely be civil war over the succession. The heir to the throne would have to face his brothers' jealousy. There would be plots at court, and even murders. Anyone who knew the secret would be in grave danger. So he decided to run away.

At dawn he began a long and hard march across the desert. Sweaty and tired, he walked under the burning sun. His tongue swelled up with thirst and his lips began to crack; there was no water for miles. On the point of giving up, his hopes were raised when he heard the sound of sheep behind a sand dune. Over the dune came strangely-dressed shepherds – Bedouin, who roamed the desert with their flocks. Their chief gave Sinhue water and food, and Sinhue joined his wandering tribe. He stayed with them until they reached Byblos, in Phoenicia.

Then Sinhue went to Syria and lived there for a year. He became well-known there, and the prince of Syria asked to see him. The prince was impressed by the Egyptian's eloquence, and realised he would be a useful source of information about Egypt. He made Sinhue tutor to his children. Sinhue married the prince's daughter, and was given a huge piece of land to grow figs, grapes, wheat and barley. He lived a life of luxury in Syria; his sons became great lords, and in war or peace his family was praised.

SINHUE COMES HOME

Sinhue's success made some people envious. A Syrian soldier came one day and challenged him to a duel. He could not refuse, although he knew it meant death for one of them. At dawn, they met in front of huge crowds. Sinhue dodged the angry Syrian's spears until all his enemy's weapons were used up. Then the Syrian threw himself towards Sinhue like a vulture on a lamb. Sinhue took his bow and shot the Syrian in the neck, then ran to the fallen man and killed him with his axe. He put his foot on the Syrian's back and gave a victory whoop to the crowd. By custom, all the Syrian's possessions were now his.

But that night Sinhue could not sleep. He was homesick for Egypt, haunted by the idea that he might have died in Syria, on foreign soil and without a proper Egyptian funeral. He wrote to the pharaoh, asking for mercy.

Many days later, a messenger came from the pharaoh, inviting Sinhue to his court. Sinhue said goodbye to his power and his lands, and headed south. A ship full of gifts awaited him.

At the Egyptian court, he fell to his knees. He heard the pharaoh speak to him in a friendly tone, and realised it was his old comrade Sesostris. Sinhue told the court his story, then the pharaoh offered him lands in Egypt. He also ordered the royal architects to build his friend a magnificent tomb. The exile had come home to perfect happiness.

Sinhue abased himself before the pharaoh.

▷ CHEOPS AND THE MAGICIAN ◁

King Cheops was bored. He called his sons and asked them to amuse him with stories about the great magicians of old. The first prince told how a magician had used his powers to find a jewel which a court lady had lost in the river. The others told more fantastic tales. Cheops was excited by the idea of the old magicians' knowledge. He longed to know the secrets of the gods! He was sad that there seemed to be no such magicians in his day.

One of his sons interrupted: 'I know a magician like those of old. His name is Jedi and he is 110 years old. But he eats like a young man: five hundred loaves and a whole ox a day, and a hundred pitchers of beer. And he is said to know one of the gods' secret numbers: the exact number of secret things hidden in Thoth's temple.'

The king listened. Numbers had magic

power, and if he knew such a secret one, he could use it for one of the measurements of the great pyramid he was having built – which would give him more magic power. He summoned Jedi to the palace, and asked the magician searching questions.

'I hear that you can put back a head that has been cut off. Is that true?'

'Absolutely true, Your Majesty.'

'I want to see. Slave, fetch a prisoner!'

'No, no, Your Majesty! Men must not be treated that way! Fetch a duck and a goose!'

The slave brought the birds, and cut off their heads. The old man put their heads back on their necks as if it was child's play. Then he did the same with a bull. Cheops, encouraged by these wonders, asked what he really wanted to know:

'I have heard that you know something about

Cheops inspects the building of his pyramid.

the mysterious objects hidden in Thoth's temple.'

'Your Majesty, I know what they are, the number of them, and where they are hidden in the temple. But I cannot bring them to you.'

'Who can, then?'

'The eldest of Reddedet's three sons.'

'Who is Reddedet?' asked the puzzled king.

'She is the wife of a priest of Ra, Your Majesty. She is expecting triplets, whose father is Ra himself. The first-born will be chief priest of his temple at Heliopolis.'

Cheops was silent. This was bad news: it meant that his own sons would not come to the throne. Ra's three sons would start a line of kings – a new dynasty.

At Reddedet's house, her husband the priest was waiting; she was near the time of birth. Suddenly he saw the ram-god Khnoum, and many goddesses, among them Isis and Nephthys. Ra had sent them to help his wife have her babies. They stayed in the house until all three were born. Isis named them, and the goddess Meskhenet told their fortunes: each in turn would be pharaoh. The goddesses gave each baby a royal crown, and bade the priest keep their destiny secret.

The grateful priest gave the god and goddesses sacks of grain. Khnoum carried them on his back. But the goddesses raised a storm by magic, as an excuse to go back to the priest. They asked him to keep the sacks, saying they would come for them soon.

Weeks later Reddedet found that her larder was short of grain. She sent her servant to take some from the sacks kept for the 'strangers'. In the granary, the servant stopped in surprise. Music was coming from the pile of sacks! She knew what this meant: it was a sign of a pharaoh's birth. The triplets would be kings.

The woman decided to keep her discovery quiet. But one day Reddedet beat her for a mistake, and in anger she threatened to tell Cheops what she knew. She did not have the chance. While she was getting water, the gods sent a crocodile to eat her up. Nothing could keep Reddedet's sons from the throne.

31

▷ MONUMENTS OF THE SUN ◁

The workmen dug away, and the huge statue came back into sight.

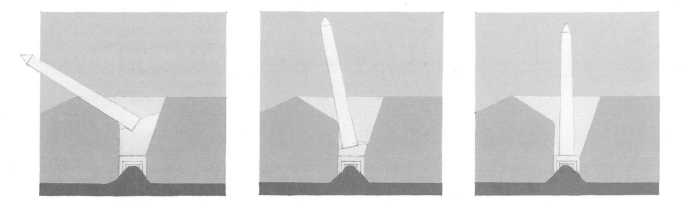

The erection of an obelisk.

Whips cracked, and tired, sweaty men flexed their muscles. Hundreds of them were pulling long ropes, at the end of which were sleds carrying enormous blocks of stone. The stone had been brought from far away in a great fleet of boats. They were building King Cheops's pyramid at Giza. Thousands of men worked here every year when the fields were flooded and there was no work to be done on the land; it was their duty to their living god. But even with all those labourers, the work had taken 17 years – and more would pass before it was finished.

Cheops's pyramid, his tomb, was the greatest of all the pyramids of Egypt. It was 147 metres high and more than 230 wide; the biggest ever built. It now seems cruel of the pharaoh to make his people work so hard for a mere tomb; but to him it was a vital matter. The pyramid itself would help him in his journey to the next world. Even its shape had a meaning: it represented the little island where Ra had hatched from his egg at the beginning of time.

LIVING STATUES

It was a dark night. A cry crossed the empty desert. In the shadow of Cheops's ancient pyramid – now flanked by his successors' tombs – Prince Tuthmosis had woken up suddenly. He had dreamed of a deep voice complaining:

'I am the Sphinx, guardian of the western lands where the sun goes at night and the dead live. I watch over the Pyramids, but I cannot see the light of day. I am suffocating under the

OBELISKS

The Egyptians were ingenious builders. They built their huge monuments with very simple tools and an enormous workforce. The raising of an obelisk, a tall stone pillar outside a temple, shows how their techniques worked. First they put the obelisk's base in position. Then they built two huge ramps to form a funnel above the base. The funnel was filled with sand. The obelisk was hauled, bottom first, up a ramp, and eased into the funnel, with its base resting on the sand. Down on the ground a hole was then dug, to let the sand out of the funnel. As the sand slowly sank away, the obelisk settled on its waiting base, and the ramps could be removed. The obelisk was so heavy that nothing could shift it from its base.

desert sand!' The dream haunted Tuthmosis. When he was king, he sent workmen to Giza. Their task was to free the Sphinx from a mountain of sand that the wind had blown over it. Slowly they dug away, and the huge statue of a lion with a man's head came back to sight. The young king had pleased the gods.

This sphinx was just the biggest of many, and all were thought to be alive. They were the protectors of the good, and the implacable enemies of the wicked. No wicked man dared go near a temple that was protected by a sphinx.

The sound of inconsolable weeping came from the scribe's house. A group of lamenting women suddenly came out and threw themselves into the street. Their heads and faces were smeared with mud. Then the men came out with deep sighs to show their sorrow. Everyone knew what this meant: Ani, the scribe and head of the family, was dead.

Ani's family had a lot of arrangements to make. First the body had to be preserved. For this, they entrusted it to an embalmer. The

Egyptians believed that everyone had a 'Ka', an invisible double. Ani's Ka had been with him since birth, and would live after his death; but to do so, it needed his body to stay undecayed. Nobody ever said, 'Ani is dead.' Instead they said 'Ani has passed to his Ka.'

To allow Ani's soul to enjoy a happy life in the next world, the embalmer had to treat his body in exactly the same way as Anubis the jackal had, long ago, preserved Osiris's body. Ani was an important man, a royal scribe, so his

The embalmers wrapped the mummy, using the techniques of Anubis.

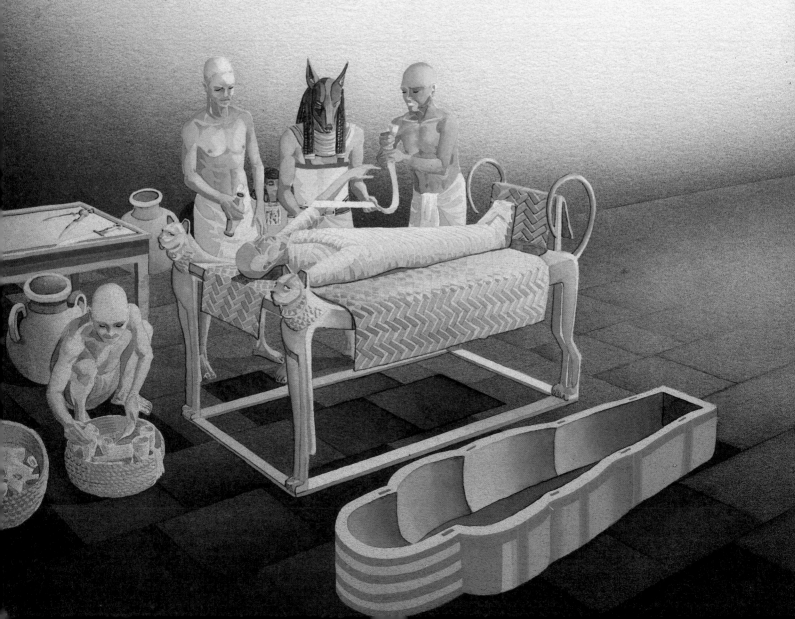

family could easily pay for the best kind of mummy. Poorer people, if they could afford to be mummified at all, had less costly treatments which did not last so well.

Ani's embalmer set to work. He gutted the body, washed it with palm wine and powdered it with spices. He filled the cavity with a mixture of aromatic plants, then stitched it up. Then he left it for 70 days in natron, a chemical which drew out all the water from the flesh. Then the body was washed and wrapped in fine linen bandages smeared with resin gathered from acacia trees.

The mummy was then returned to the family, who had meanwhile ordered a sarcophagus of richly decorated wood. On its cover was a portrait of Ani. The mummy was placed inside, to wait for a while standing at the entrance of the tomb.

ROAD TO ANOTHER WORLD

The funeral service was solemn. A priest performed the rite of opening the mouth, so that Ani could speak in the next world. Then the sarcophagus was laid in the tomb, where everything Ani would need was provided. If Ani's Ka could not eat it might die again – this time for good. So the tomb was supplied with food, furniture, and other useful things. The tomb's walls were covered with paintings. Some showed the gods who would help and protect Ani on his journey through the next world to Osiris's land. Others showed hunting scenes. Around the tomb were little statues called Shabtis. They held hoes, and they would take Ani's place when he was ordered to work in Osiris's fields.

The Ka would have to travel a long and dangerous road to reach Osiris's happy kingdom. To guide it on its way, Ani's family gave him his own Book of The Dead: a roll of papyrus, with pictures of the many places the soul would pass. The text told Ani all the spells he would need, and the right answers to difficult questions which would be asked to test him on the way.

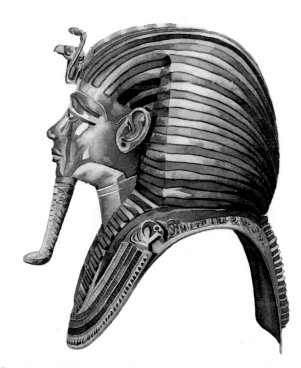

The pharaoh Tutankhamun wore this gold mask in his coffin.

The mummy was placed in a coffin painted with the portrait of the dead person inside it.

A funeral chamber excavated at Thebes.

▷A SOUL'S JOURNEY◁

With an angry hiss, the serpent raised its threatening head and threw itself on Ani. A frightening moment, but Ani, without fear or hesitation, spoke the words which would save him. 'Away, Serpent! Geb and Shu are at your side! Eat mice and rats, in honour of Ra!' At once the monster withdrew.

Ani's journey to the next world was full of terrors and obstacles. His funeral barge had already travelled a great distance, and met many dangers. But the Book of the Dead his family had placed near his mummy was a constant help. There he found the spells which allowed him to pass all the difficult tests the gods imposed. If he failed even one, Ani would die for a second time and disappear for ever. The idea terrified him, but bravely he went on towards the place of judgement, where he would have to give an exact account of his life.

Resting after his trial with the monster, Ani remembered how he had first entered the underworld. At that solemn moment, he had to identify certain spirits. He managed it easily with the book's help. The book had also helped him find the green lake where Osiris had been washed on the day of his birth. He had also had to give the right name to each of the gates he passed through. After these tests, Ani saw a tree with rich green foliage. In its shade a bloody battle was in progress. A cat, with its fur bristling and its claws out, was fighting off a snake from the black abyss. The cat's sharp claws ripped the terrifying reptile's head. There was more to the fight than met the eye: it was a riddle, another test.

Ani passed the test: he recognized the god Ra. Before his eyes Ra triumphed over his sworn enemy, the hideous serpent Apopis, master of the shadows. By naming the two enemies, Ani had won the right to call on the scarab Khephri, the rising sun, when he needed protection and assistance.

Next he saw Ouadjyt, the cobra-goddess, mistress of fire, twined around a bed of lotus flowers. The goddess lifted her head, and he saw how her neck was swollen with anger against the powers of the night and the enemies of Ra. She was Ani's friend and supporter, and gave him strength to continue the journey. Ani thanked her and left to face the next test.

He confidently named all the guardians who watched the seven castles and the ten gates of the underworld and went on. Soon he found himself before the god Thoth, easy to recognize because of his ibis head. Thoth was bright blue, the colour of the precious stone lapis lazuli. To gain the right to speak to the god, Ani had to call the six first guardians of the ten gates. Ani remembered them all. Now he had to address a long speech to Thoth.

Ani was introduced to the gods of the principal sacred cities of Egypt. Then he begged Thoth at great length to let him repeat the mysterious words which made new life possible. From the jackal Anubis, he claimed a new heart. Then he asked the gods to give him air. He prayed desperately not to die a second time, and asked for the right to return to earth, invisible, to see his home again.

Now the dreadful shape of Apopis loomed in front of Ani. Ani needed all his courage as, just like Ra, he fought the monster, whose gigantic body moved with terrifying speed. With the gods' help Ani defeated Apopis. Then he sang hymns to Ra, Osiris and Thoth, and spoke magic spells to transform himself into many different creatures and gods. First he became a swift and gracious falcon of gold, which whirled high up in the sky, then the great snake Sito whose coils encircled the world. Then in turn, he changed into the god Ptah, then a ram, a heron and a lotus. Each transformation enabled him to overcome a different obstacle.

The end of the journey was near. Ani came to the door of a colossal room. Inside he could see immense pillars decorated with lotus flowers. Ani prepared for the supreme test. The hour of judgement had come!

ANI'S SOUL FLIES ABOVE HIS MUMMY ON ITS BED

THE TOMB IS OPENED FOR ANI'S SOUL & IN THE SHADOW OF OSIRIS...

ANI CAN GO TO EARTH AND SEE HIS HOUSE. HE DEFEATS THE SERPENT APOPIS.

▷ THE GARDENS OF OSIRIS ◁

Struck with wonder and terror, Ani dared not move. Through the door he could see a huge and solemn crowd in the vast and shadowy room. Along the sides, silent and terrible, stood the 42 demons of Hell. At the far end, half-visible in the dark shadows, sat Osiris on his magnificent throne. Ani could just see the sceptre and flail he held, signs of royal power. Behind him, Isis and Nephthys watched the poor soul at the door.

In the middle of the room Anubis was checking a huge set of scales; he could not risk the least error. Thoth waited nearby to write down Osiris's verdict. Horus was the judge's clerk.

WEIGHING THE HEART

A gracious young woman, wearing an ostrich feather headdress, came towards Ani. She was Maat, daughter of Ra, goddess of truth, order and justice. She played an important part in Egyptian life; the pharaoh consulted her about all his decisions, and ordinary people said that a sincere person 'spoke like Maat'.

She joined Ani by the door and invited him to address a prayer to Osiris. The dead man hailed the great god, king of this world, the ever-good. He then began to plead his innocence by listing all the sins and wicked acts he had not committed. When he had finished, Maat pushed him quickly to the middle of the room, near the scales. On the right-hand pan of the scales was an ostrich feather, representing Maat. Anubis seized Ani's heart and placed it in the other pan.

This was the moment of truth; woe to Ani if his heart was heavier than the feather of truth, showing he had not lived a good life! If it were, he would be given to a monster, the Devourer, which impatiently waited at Thoth's feet. It had a crocodile's head, and the front of its body was like a lion and the back like a hippopotamus. It would gobble up a wicked man in seconds.

Ani was more anxious than ever before. Horus looked at the scales, then told Thoth the verdict. Anubis told the audience that this man Ani had led a spotless life. The disappointed Devourer withdrew to wait for the next soul.

Ani had got through this trial, but could not leave yet. First he had to speak to all the 42 demons, calling each by its own name, and once again list the sins he had not committed. The slightest error or falsehood meant he would never know eternal life. Worse, if a slip of memory made him forget one demon's name or confuse it with another's, the deeply offended demon would eat him up on the spot.

Luckily Ani's memory was good. The judges let him go to Osiris's throne to say a humble prayer. Now he could go on to the happy lands of the West, his new home.

LANDS OF THE WEST

Ani had been through the sad adventure of death, and shown he was worthy of eternal life. He would never again be hungry, thirsty or in pain. He could walk about among the stars or rest under shady sycamore trees, drinking the sky-goddess Nut's tasty milk. The fertile soil grew delicious food.

All the dead people had the jobs they had had on earth: the peasant had his hoe, the pharaoh his throne. But in Osiris's land nobody was poor or ill, as so many living people were. Eternal life was just like home, but never spoilt by any trouble. Ani still worked hard as a scribe.

Maat leads Ani to the weighing-scales.

EGYPTIAN GODS

Ancient Egypt lasted for three thousand years, and it is not surprising that people's beliefs changed in all that time. Every town had its own god or goddess, and a famous god in one place might be unknown in the rest of the country. Over the years, as the power of the pharaohs grew, local gods might be brought into the national religion, and one god might be explained as an aspect of another. The sun god's old local names were kept as names for him at different times of day: Khephri at dawn, Ra when he was at his strongest at noon, and Atum as he faded into the West. But the Pharaoh worshipped him at Thebes under the name Amon-Ra. All the hawk gods were united in the figure of Horus.

Ra, Isis, Osiris and Horus were the greatest gods of Egypt, but many others played their part. Here are some of them:

———————————◇———————————

Amon: Worshipped at Thebes, he became the great god of Egypt in the New Kingdom, and his priests then were among the most powerful people in the land. Sometimes shown with a human head, sometimes a ram's.

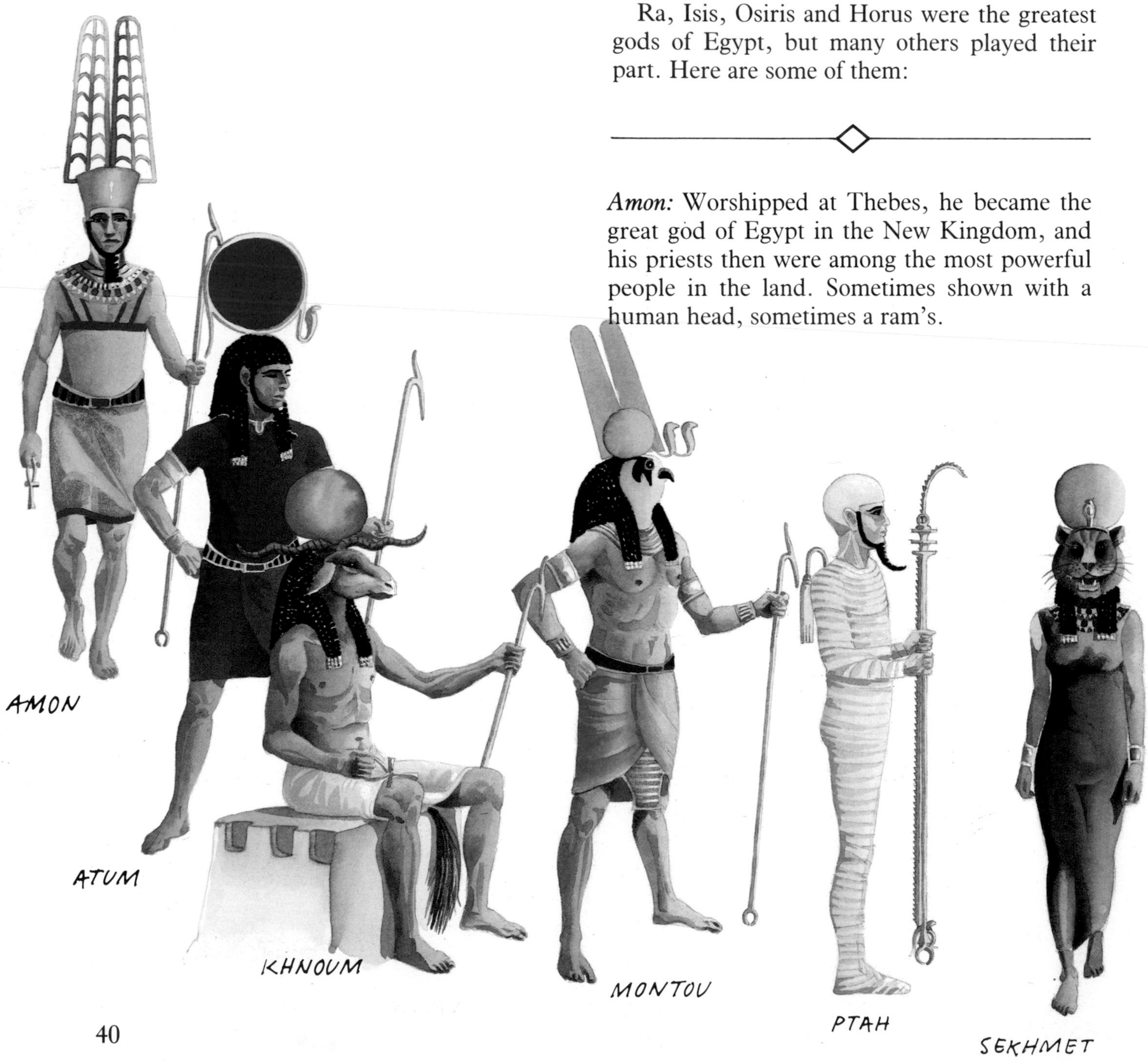

AMON

ATUM

KHNOUM

MONTOU

PTAH

SEKHMET

Atum: The sun-god worshipped at Heliopolis.

Khnoum: A ram-god, whose main temple was on the island of Elephantine.

Montou: A warrior god with a falcon's head, worshipped at Thebes.

Ptah: Protector of craftsmen, and pictured as a mummy. He was thought to listen attentively to human prayers, and is sometimes shown with extra-large ears beside him!

Sekhmet: The lioness goddess, feared and worshipped in many places. She sent the messengers of death, and was responsible for plagues.

Bastet: A kind goddess with a cat's head, whose temple was at Bubastis.

Bes: An ugly little god of the people, who protected lovers and sleepers. He drove away reptiles and evil spirits.

Tauret: The hippopotamus goddess, who helped pregnant women.

Neith: The people of Sais believed this goddess created the world. She was a good archer, and fought off evil spirits.

Sobek: The crocodile god who ruled the Fayum region from his city of Crocodilopolis.

Khonshu: A magician and god of the moon. The Thebans said he was the son of Amon-Ra.

BASTET

BES

TAURET

NEITH

SOBEK

KHONSHU

41

⊳ SACRED ANIMALS ⊲

The first stone struck the stranger's head. He fell, badly hurt, as more stones rained down. All around an angry crowd shouted. The poor man could not remember doing anything wrong. He was paying with his life for a crime he was unaware of – accidentally killing a cat.

Such events were common, because in Egypt, the cat was a god. If a house caught fire the people might abandon their furnture, but would run back into the flames to save a cat. When a cat died, the people of the house shaved their eyebrows as a sign of mourning. In the cat-goddess Bast's sanctuary at Bubastis, archaeologists have found thousands of mummified cats.

Many other animals were worshipped, and thought to be living gods. Foreign visitors were astonished to see lavish funerals given to a bull, when Apis, a bull called the 'magnificent soul' of the god Ptah, died at his temple in Memphis. After Apis died, priests searched the land for a bull with the same markings.

Wild animals were also honoured. Lions were often pictured in temples, as themselves, or as a creature called a sphinx, with a lion's body and a human face.

A bird called the phoenix was worshipped at sunrise in Heliopolis. If it perched on the city's sacred willow tree, it meant good fortune. 'The

42

phoenix is returned!' people cried joyfully. Children born on such a day were named in honour of the event.

In the last centuries of Ancient Egypt, vast animal cemeteries were built. At Thoth's town, Hermopolis, huge numbers of mummified ibises and baboons have been found. Falcons, dogs, rams, snakes, fish and even, at Hermopolis, two ostriches were mummified and buried in state.

Some animals raised more mixed feelings. The savage crocodile, enemy of humans, and an ally of Seth, was treated as master of the universe in one region. At the town of Crocodilopolis, hundreds were served, fed and adored by a throng of priests. The hippopotamus was also sometimes seen as an enemy of mankind, but in the form of Tauret, protector of pregnant women, it was loved. Amulets in Tauret's shape had magic power. There were even friendly snakes, such as Ouadjyt or hostile ones such as Apopis.

The most famous sacred animal is perhaps the scarab, a beetle which pushes along a ball of dung. It was seen as the god 'who came into existence alone'. Its red ball of dung was Khephri, the rising sun. Amulets and jewels showing it often have mottoes, such as 'The peace of the soul is better than anger', or 'Amon is master of my life'. Others bore the pharaoh's name, which had magic power.

MEDITERRANEAN SEA

ROSETTA
ALEXANDRIA
BUTO
MENDES
SAIS
TANIS
BUBASTIS

GIZA
ABOUSIR
SAKKARA
DAHSHOUR
HELIOPOLIS
MEMPHIS

CROCODILOPOLIS

HERMOPOLIS
ARMANA

RED SEA

ABYDOS
COPTOS
VALLEY OF THE KINGS
THEBES
KARNAK
LUXOR

OMBOS

ELEPHANTINE

ABU SIMBEL

▷ BEHIND THE LEGENDS ◁

Ancient Egypt was very important in the history of civilisation. The country owed everything to the River Nile, the longest river in the world at 6700 kilometres from its source to the sea. Without it, Egypt would be as barren as the Sahara desert. But because it made a narrow strip of land fertile, the Egyptians were able to develop a great civilisation.

The Inundation, the great annual floods which left rich mud when they receded, occurred in late summer, when the snow on top of the mountains of Ethiopia melted, sending huge amounts of water down the river. The Egyptians invented clever systems of canals and dams, to bring the water into the fields and keep it after the floods had passed.

A long history

The beginning of Egyptian civilisation came about 3200 BC. Little is known about the early times. Old legends suggest that at first there were two countries, Upper and Lower Egypt, which were united in about 2900 BC. Egypt remained an independent country until the Romans conquered it in 30 BC.

Historians divide this long history into four periods: The Old Kingdom, the Middle Kingdom, the New Kingdom and the Ptolemaic Period (named after the Ptolemies, rulers of the time, who were of Greek ancestry). The three 'Kingdoms' represent long periods of stable government – interrupted by wars or other disturbances. The long time-scale is further divided into 27 dynasties, each representing a family of pharaohs.

Life in Egypt changed a lot during 3000 years, but there was a continuity about it; religion changed over the years, but (except in the short reign of Akhenaten, the rebel king), the change was always gradual. The same was true of everyday life, and of the role of the pharaoh. Even the Ptolemies, who are regarded now as weak, decadent and a mere shadow of the old Pharaohs, thought of themselves as inheritors of a great tradition. The last of them was Cleopatra VII, known to all the world as just Cleopatra. In his play *Antony and Cleopatra*, William Shakespeare describes her riding down the Nile on her golden barge, to meet the Roman conqueror Antony:

> The barge she sat in, like a burnished throne,
> Burned on the water. The poop was beaten gold;
> Purple the sails, and so perfumed that
> The winds were love-sick with them; the oars were silver,
> Which to the tune of flutes gave stroke . . .

Shakespeare took his description from a Roman author, who lived a century after Cleopatra's death.

Land of mysteries
For all the people of ancient times, Egypt was a land of fascinating secrets. In the 5th century BC the Greek author Herodotus wrote down many of their legends, and he is the source for some of the stories in this book. Until the 1800s AD, all our knowledge of Egyptian life came from Greek and Roman authors, because many Ancient Egyptian buildings were covered with sand, and nobody could read their writing. All sorts of strange things were believed about Egypt in the Renaissance, based on Greek texts and garbled accounts of the buildings which could still be seen. By then, Egypt was an Arab land, and its people were devout Muslims, who did not approve of their predecessors' worship of 'idols'.

All that changed in 1799, when the French general Napoleon was fighting the British in Egypt. Soldiers digging a trench at Rosetta found a large black stone, with three inscriptions. One was in Egyptian hieroglyphics – the picture-writing used for religious and official texts – one in everyday writing called 'demotic', and another in Greek! This meant

Alexandria: Founded by the Greek king Alexander the Great in 332 BC, this was the capital of Egypt in Ptolemaic times. It held a great library and was a centre of learning in the ancient world.

Rosetta: A Delta port, where the stone which held the key to Egyptian writing was found.

Buto: An important town in Egyptian mythology, where Horus was brought up by the cobra-goddess.

Sais: Sacred city of the goddess Neith.

Tanis: Site of the only royal tombs to be found intact, apart from Tutankhamun's.

Bubastis: 'City of Bast', the cat-goddess; great cemeteries of mummified cats have been found here.

Heliopolis: 'City of the sun', a great religious centre, but few remains survive.

Memphis: A royal city, dedicated to the god Ptah. Probably the biggest city of Ancient Egypt.

Giza: Site of three pharaohs' pyramids, the Great Sphinx, and many other tombs of lesser people.

Abousir: Site of a 5th Dynasty pyramid.

Sakkara: A great cemetery, containing the very earliest pyramids – which had stepped sides.

Dahshour: More pyramids, one of which is an unusual shape.

Crocodilopolis: City and temple of the crocodile-god Sobek.

Hermopolis: Thoth's city and temple.

Armana (Akhetaton): Founded by the rebel king Akhenaten in about 1362, in honour of his one god Aten, this city was destroyed after his death.

Abydos: A very ancient city. Osiris's head was believed to be buried here.

Dendera: Site of a great temple dedicated to Hathor.

Ombos (Kom Ombo): Temple of Sobek.

Coptos: Site of three temples to Isis and Osiris.

Karnak: A huge group of temples to the north of Thebes, where Amon-Ra was worshipped.

Thebes: Capital of Egypt after about 2000 BC. Site of the royal palace and a temple to Amon-Ra, and near the Valley of the Kings.

Luxor: Another great temple to Amon-Ra.

Elephantine: An island city in the Nile, with a temple to the god Khnoum.

Abu Simbel: Site of huge temples to Amon-Ra and the pharaoh Rameses II, and Hathor and the pharaoh's wife Nefertari, which were moved when the Aswan dam was built.

that scholars could begin to decode the Ancient Egyptian language.

The British and the French competed to discover Egyptian remains, and many mummies, grave-goods, and Egyptian statues can be seen today at the British Museum in London and the Louvre in Paris. The British Museum has the original of Ani's *Book of the Dead*, and the Rosetta Stone.

Tomb of treasure
Though Western scholars only began to discover the riches of Egypt in the 1800s, many people had explored their tombs before the archaeologists got there – looking for treasure. Grave-robbing was even a problem for the Ancient Egyptians, since tombs were often full of rich goods and jewellery – especially royal tombs. The Old Kingdom pharaohs

built secret passages into their pyramids, to make it as hard as possible for thieves to enter. Once the Romans, and then the Arabs, had conquered Egypt, and the old religion was forgotten, there was little but the builders' own tricks to stop people ransacking the tombs. Even mummies were stolen – their dried flesh was thought to have medicinal power, and was also used as a painter's pigment – for flesh tones! Paintings and statues survived in the tombs that were excavated, but no pharaoh's tomb, with all its rich goods, was found intact.

New Kingdom pharaohs were buried in the Valley of the Kings, in tombs cut into the wall of a cliff. Many of the tombs were robbed in ancient times; priests sometimes had to move the mummies to secret

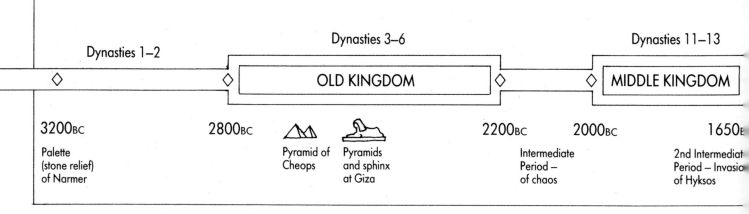

Dynasties 1–2		Dynasties 3–6			Dynasties 11–13
◇	◇	OLD KINGDOM	◇	◇	MIDDLE KINGDOM
3200BC	2800BC			2200BC	2000BC	1650B
Palette (stone relief) of Narmer		Pyramid of Cheops	Pyramids and sphinx at Giza	Intermediate Period – of chaos	2nd Intermediat Period – Invasio of Hyksos